THE THREE MILE WALK

Study Guide | Five Sessions

BANNING LIEBSCHER

with Beth Graybill

THE THREE-MILE WALK

Study Guide | Five Sessions

CLAIMING THE COURAGE TO LIVE
YOUR GOD-GIVEN CALLING

ZONDERVAN
BOOKS

The Three-Mile Walk Study Guide

© 2020 Banning Liebscher

This title is also available as a Zondervan ebook. Visit www.zondervan.com/ebooks.

Requests for information should be addressed to:
3900 *Sparks Dr. SE, Grand Rapids, Michigan,* 49546.

ISBN 978-0-310-12055-1 (softcover)
ISBN 978-0-310-12056-8 (ebook)

20 21 22 23 24 DSC 10 9 8 7 6 5 4 3 2 1

Contents

Introduction

Welcome to *The Three-Mile Walk Study Guide* experience. Over the course of five teaching sessions in this study, we're going to draw a few important lessons from the life of Jonathan and his armor-bearer found in 1 Samuel 14. We will see how their three-mile journey through the Valley of Mikmash—a treacherous canyon trail between two military camps—carries a profound metaphor for followers of Jesus today. Although the two young soldiers were embroiled in a seemingly losing battle with the Philistines while the rest of their hopeless comrades were camped out under a tree, they had the courage to fight the enemy and believe God would back them up. But they had to be willing to traverse the treacherous terrain before they could step into battle and see God bring about the impossible victory.

Here's the reason why I think this story is a story for all of us. Like the Israelite army in 1 Samuel 14, many believers in the church today are "hopelessly camped out" and not engaging the call of God on their lives. And yet, God is still awakening dreamers like Jonathan and his armor-bearer—men and women who are discontented with the idea of remaining hopeless under a tree. These dreamers are tired of staying passive about the problems they see, and they sense God stirring something in their hearts. The courage of these dreamers reminds us that God calls us to be like Jesus—to overcome evil with good and do the impossible as we seek his kingdom here on earth. The question for all of us who identify as dreamers is whether we will open our hearts to dream *with* God. Are we willing to become filled with the same divine discontent and engage in pursuing God's call on our lives with a bold "yes"? This kind of "yes" communicates that we are willing to take full ownership of this calling and refuse to settle for anything less.

But once we decide to engage our calling, we still have a journey ahead of us. And three important milestones lie along the journey. In fact, Jonathan's three-mile journey represented these three key areas of character transformation required to fulfill our calling: *holiness*, *courage*, and *faith*. My hope in this study is to bring a fresh perspective, timeless insight, and practical instruction for growing in each one of these areas. I'm excited we're on this journey together. Let's get started.

—Banning Liebscher

How to Use This Guide

The Three-Mile Walk video study is designed to be experienced in a group setting such as a Bible study, Sunday school class, or any small group gathering. Each session begins with a welcome section, several questions to get you thinking about the topic, and a reading from the Bible. You will then watch a video with Banning Liebscher and engage in some small-group discussion. You will close each session with a time of personal reflection and prayer as a group.

Each person in the group should have his or her own copy of this study guide. You are also encouraged to have a copy of *The Three-Mile Walk* book, as reading the book alongside the curriculum will provide you with deeper insights and make the journey more meaningful, especially for your professional context. (See the "For Next Week" section at the end of each between-studies section for the chapters in the book that correspond to material you and your group are discussing.)

To get the most out of your group experience, keep the following points in mind. First, the real growth in this study will happen during your small-group time. This is where you will process the content of the teaching for the week, ask questions, and learn from others as you hear what God is doing in their lives. For this reason, it is important for you to be fully committed to the group and attend each session so you can build trust and rapport with the other members. If you choose to only go through the motions, or if you refrain from participating, there is a lesser chance you will find what you're looking for during this study.

Second, remember the goal of your small group is to serve as a place where people can share, learn about God, and build intimacy and friendship. For this reason, seek to make your group a safe place. This means being honest about your thoughts and feelings and listening carefully to everyone else's opinion. (If you are a group leader, there are additional instructions and resources in the back of the book for leading a productive discussion group.)

Third, resist the temptation to fix a problem someone might be having or to correct his or her theology, as that's not the purpose of your small-group time. Also, keep everything your group shares confidential. This will foster a rewarding sense of community in your group and create a place where people can heal, be challenged, and grow spiritually.

Following your group time, reflect on the material you've covered by engaging in any or all between-sessions activities. For each session, you may wish to complete the personal study all in one sitting or spread it out over a few days (for example, working on it a half-hour a day on different days that week). Note that if you are unable to finish (or even start!) your between-sessions personal study, you should still attend the group study video session. You are still wanted and welcome at the group even if you don't have your "homework" done.

Keep in mind the videos, discussion questions, and activities are simply meant to kick-start your imagination so that you are not only open to what God wants you to hear but also how to apply it to your life. As you go through this study, be watching for what God is saying to you as you take steps forward on the journey of claiming the courage to live your God-given calling.

Note: If you are a group leader, there are additional resources provided in the back of this guide to help you lead your group members through the study.

AWAKENED TO THE CALL

PAY ATTENTION TO THE

THINGS THAT MOVE YOU

BECAUSE THEY REVEAL THE

THINGS IN YOUR HEART.

—Banning Liebscher

WELCOME

Do you remember dreaming as a kid about who or what you wanted to be when you grew up? I actually get a kick out of remembering all of the different things my eight-year-old-self wanted for my forty-year-old-self: to be a police officer like my dad, or a baseball player, or a sports broadcaster. And one of my favorite things about the journey of parenting was listening to my kids do the same when they were little. Ellie was convinced she was going to play in the WNBA, Raya wanted to be an astronaut, and my son, Lake, loves basketball and playing video games.

As we grow older, the dreams of our childhood start to take a different shape as they are influenced by our experience of the world around us. I'm sure most of us remember a few naysayers who said we couldn't be the astronaut or biologist or athlete we wanted to be, and the cheerleaders who encouraged even the slightest pursuit of an interest (*the kind of people who thought the chess club flyer they found in your backpack meant you were going to be the next world champion of chess*). But let's not forget that our dreams have also been influenced by our experience of God, who has been patiently pursuing every opportunity to awaken our hearts to his dreams for us and his call on our lives.

Can you recall moments where your heart was awakened by God and moved by his desires or dreams for your life? I can think of several moments in my life when that happened, like reading powerful biographies as a seventeen-year-old, or listening to certain preachers in my late teens, and having words spoken over me in my early twenties from others who were seeing and sensing God's call on my life. At the time, I didn't have words for those experiences, I just knew something had awakened in me—something I could not ignore. Almost two decades after those defining moments in my life, I'm convinced that what matters more than the moments of being awakened to God's dreams for our lives, is what we actually *do* with those dreams. This is what changes the trajectory of our lives. *But how do we know what to do?*

Jonathan, the son of King Saul, and his armor-bearer give us a healthy example in 1 Samuel of what it looks like to thoughtfully engage God's call on our lives by *owning the call, dreaming of the call, counting the cost of the call*, and *moving forward with the call*. Jonathan and his armor-bearer refuse to settle for anything less than *who* God wants them to be and *what* he wants them to do. My hope is that this session, inspired by Jonathan's story, encourages you to live your best life by fully engaging God's call on your life. It's time for you to stand up and move toward changing the world by stepping out on your *three-mile walk*, even when it seems like everything is at stake. Are you with me?

SHARE

If you or any of your group members are just getting to know one another, take a few minutes to introduce yourselves. Then, to kick things off, discuss one of the following questions:

- How have you experienced a defining moment that changed the trajectory of your life?

— *or* —

- When was the last time you sensed God was awakening something inside of you?

READ

Invite someone to read aloud the following passage. Listen for fresh insights as you hear the verses being read, and then discuss the questions that follow. We're starting with the backstory in 1 Samuel 13, so we understand the context of Jonathan's *three-mile walk* in 1 Samuel 14.

The Backstory

Saul was thirty years old when he became king, and he reigned over Israel forty-two years. Saul chose three thousand men from Israel; two thousand were with him at Mikmash and in the hill country of Bethel, and a thousand were with Jonathan at Gibeah in Benjamin. The rest of the men he sent back to their homes. Jonathan attacked the Philistine outpost at Geba, and the Philistines heard about it. Then Saul had the trumpet blown throughout the land and said, "Let the Hebrews hear!" So all Israel heard the news: "Saul has attacked the Philistine outpost, and now Israel has become obnoxious to the Philistines." And the people were summoned to join Saul at Gilgal. The Philistines assembled to fight Israel, with three thousand chariots, six thousand charioteers, and soldiers as numerous as the sand on the seashore. They went up and camped at Mikmash, east of Beth Aven. When the Israelites saw that their situation was critical and that their army was hard pressed, they hid in caves and thickets, among the rocks, and in pits and cisterns. Some Hebrews even crossed the Jordan to the land of Gad and Gilead. Saul remained at Gilgal, and all the troops with him were quaking with fear. He waited seven days, the time set by Samuel; but Samuel did not come to Gilgal, and Saul's men began to scatter. So he said, "Bring me the burnt offering and the fellowship offerings." And Saul offered up the burnt offering. Just as he finished making the offering, Samuel arrived, and Saul went out to greet him. "What have you done?" asked Samuel. Saul replied, "When I saw that the men were scattering, and that you did not come at the set time, and that the Philistines were assembling at Mikmash, I thought, 'Now the Philistines will come down against me at Gilgal, and I have not sought the LORD's favor.' So I felt compelled to offer the burnt offering." "You have done a foolish thing," Samuel said. "You have not kept the command the LORD your God gave you; if you had, he would have established your kingdom over Israel for all time. But now your kingdom will not endure; the LORD has sought out a man after his own heart and appointed him ruler of his people, because you have not kept the LORD's command." Then Samuel left Gilgal and went up to Gibeah in Benjamin, and Saul counted the men who were with him. They numbered about six hundred. Saul and his son Jonathan and the men with them were staying in Gibeah in Benjamin, while the Philistines camped at Mikmash. Raiding parties went out from the Philistine camp in three detachments. One turned toward Ophrah in the vicinity of Shual, another toward Beth Horon, and the third toward the borderland overlooking the Valley of Zeboyim facing the wilderness. Not a blacksmith could be found in the whole land of Israel, because the Philistines had said, "Otherwise the Hebrews will make swords or spears!" So all Israel went down to the Philistines to have their plow points, mattocks, axes and sickles sharpened. The price was two-thirds of a shekel for sharpening plow points and mattocks, and a third of a shekel for sharpening forks and axes and for repointing goads. So on the day of the battle not a soldier with Saul and Jonathan had a sword or spear in his hand; only Saul and his son Jonathan had them. Now a detachment of Philistines had gone out to the pass at Mikmash. (1 Samuel 13)

What do you notice in this passage? Name one key insight.

Imagine you are Saul or Jonathan. What would be going through your mind in this moment?

WATCH

Play the video for session one. As you watch, use the following outline to record any thoughts or concepts that stand out to you.

Notes

Defining Moments

Every believer has a call on their life:

1. The call to *be someone*.
2. The call to *do something*.

Get off the sideline: be fully engaged.

———

The three-mile walk: Jonathan and his armor-bearer.

> "Do all that you have in mind," his armor-bearer said. "Go ahead; I am with you heart and soul." (1 Samuel 14:7)

God Is Awakening You with Dreams in Your Heart

Knowing those dreams.
Engaging in those dreams.
Moving forward.
God calls us to do the impossible.

———

Childlike ability to dream.
Jonathan and his armor-bearer.

> " . . .Nothing can hinder the LORD from saving, whether by many or by few." (1 Samuel 14:6)

With God All *Things Are Possible*

> Jesus looked at them and said, "With man this is impossible, but with God all things are possible." (Matthew 19:26)

———

Start dreaming again. Who is God calling you to be?

———

God's invitation: *the three-mile walk.*

DISCUSS

Take a few minutes with your group members to discuss what you just watched and explore these concepts in Scripture.

1. How are you actively engaging in the dreams God has placed on your heart?

2. Has there ever been a time when you shut down your dreams because of disappointment or because they seemed impossible?

3. **Read 1 Samuel 14:1–7.** Jonathan and his armor-bearer had to take a treacherous three-mile walk to follow God. Yet not all journeys with God are treacherous. How would you describe the "three-mile walk" God wants you to take with him?

4. Who is God calling you to *be*? What is God calling you to *do*?

5. Are there a few experiences, thoughts, or feelings in your life lately that point to the idea that God is trying to awaken something in you right now?

VALLEY OF MIKMASH

(Also known as Michmash, Machmas, Micmas, and Mukhmas)

The Arab village of Mukhmas preserves the name of the biblical city of Michmash. The town sat next to "the pass" mentioned twice in Scripture and apparently served to keep an eye on this important route. Michmash was settled throughout the period of the monarchy, as it was mentioned in the account of Saul and Jonathan and later in a prophecy of Isaiah. Michmash was near the border between Benjamin and Ephraim, and thus near the border of the northern and southern kingdoms, probably belonging to Israel most of the time. The hill country is deeply cut by deep canyons (wadis) that run east-west. These significantly restrict traffic to the ridges above the wadis, making passage north-south difficult except on the central watershed ridge. Consequently, this route is noted in Scripture on several occasions. The pass is also mentioned in connection with Jonathan's attack on the Philistines (1 Sam. 14). Saul's son surprised the Philistine garrison by not coming across the pass, but instead going around and climbing up and down steep cliffs. These cliffs were named Seneh and Bozez. When the Philistines saw Jonathan and his armor-bearer climbing up, they called to them to continue, thus signaling to Jonathan that God was with them. Jonathan's defeat of this contingent led to a national victory that day. (https://www.bibleplaces.com/michmash/)

6. **Read Matthew 19:16–30.** What invitation(s) did Jesus extend to the young man and to his own disciples? How does this passage influence your perspective on God's call to you?

RESPOND

Briefly review the outline for the video teaching and any notes you took. In the space below, write down the most significant point you took away from this session

Is there a specific action step you can take this week to move toward the dream or desire God is inviting you into right now?

PRAY

Close your time together by praying for each other. Pray that God would give you clarity on what it looks like to pursue his dreams, his desires, and his vision for your life. And if you already have that clarity, ask God for the wisdom and courage to keep moving forward on your journey from a healthy place. Write down any specific prayer requests in the space below so you can remember to continue praying throughout the week.

1

SESSION

—

Maybe you're sitting here with your study guide thinking, "This is a great story, Banning, but I'm not Jonathan and my life looks *way different* than this ancient guy and his armor-bearer." You're right. You're not Jonathan. You are *you*. But I still think you can learn a few powerful lessons about the way Jonathan responded to God—lessons that will make a difference in the way you pursue your dreams and desires too. And I believe the work you do here as an individual between each session is just as important as the work you are doing together in your group. My hope for you is that you start to live your best life engaged in God's call on your life, and I think Jonathan's response in 1 Samuel 14 provides a helpful framework for your response. Jonathan moved through four internal postures or attitudes that shaped the way he engaged in God's call on his life. He *took ownership* of his call; he *dreamed* about his call; he *counted the cost* of his call; and he was *provoked* to keep moving forward with his call. I believe these same four postures can be applicable and true in your life too.

DAY 1: OWNING THE CALL ON YOUR LIFE

In order to awaken to the call on our lives, we have to take some ownership of that call. I believe God's call has two dimensions for every single one of us—*identity* and *mission*. There's the call of who we are to *be* (identity), and the call of what we are to *do* (mission). The first call is relational identity—God is calling us to be someone, and that someone is a son or daughter of God *and* an image-bearer of God. This is our identity. And out of that identity comes our mission—the work we are called to *do*. But it's important to remember that our mission is connected to the corporate mission of the people of God. We are all called to partner with God, individually and collectively, to impact the world with the saving freedom of the gospel and the reality of God's kingdom.

1. **Read Genesis 1:26–31.** What does it mean to be an image-bearer of God? How does this idea affect God's call on our lives?

2. Revisit your answers to the group discussion questions for session one. How did you answer the question, "Who is God calling you to *be*? What is God calling you to *do*?"

3. In his book, *The Three-Mile Walk*, Banning says, "Ownership [over our calling] is a mindset that generates an attitude of authority, initiative, and responsibility." (pages 12–13)

How would you rate the *attitude of authority* you have over your calling on a scale of 1–5? Does it really feel like yours? If not, what can you do or think to make it feel like your dream, your calling?

4. How would you rate the steps of *initiative* you've taken in response to your calling, using that same 1–5 scale? Where are you initiating action as a result of your calling, or where could you be taking more initiative?

5. How would you rate the sense of *responsibility* you feel toward your calling? What are you doing with the responsibility you feel, or what could you be doing with your responsibility?

6. What will be lost if you don't take ownership of your calling? And how does that loss potentially impact the world around you?

7. **Read Ephesians 4:1–16.** The term *ownership* may mean something different for each one of us based on our life experiences. How does this passage describe a healthy perspective of ownership regarding God's calling on our lives?

8. Which areas of healthy ownership, as they appear in Ephesians 4, are currently being reflected in your life as it relates to your calling? And where do you have room for growth?

9. How have you been relying on others—your pastor, leader, boss, parent, spouse, coach, teacher—to carry the responsibility of ownership for God's call on your life? And how will you reclaim your own responsibility?

10. Who is your "armor-bearer"? Who is the friend or mentor who will walk alongside you and encourage you to take ownership of God's call on your life?

Read Ephesians 4:17–32. The apostle Paul goes on to give his readers, the Ephesians, a few helpful instructions regarding Christian living. Consider how these instructions are still applicable to your life today as you live out God's calling in areas of both *identity* and *mission*. Think about how these instructions influence who you are and the way you show up in the world around you. And consider how these instructions influence your actions and the way you move forward with the dreams and desires God has placed on your heart. Spend a few moments in silent meditation or prayer as you reflect on your God-given identity and your God-given mission, the two dimensions of your God-given call. And don't be afraid to ask God for the courage to start owning your call with a renewed sense of confidence and clarity.

DAY 2: DREAMING OF THE CALL

We've all had a reality check when it comes to our dreams and desires, right? The desire to serve God in some interesting, unique way or in some exotic place—when reality looks like showing up to our nine-to-five job and coming home to a similar routine most nights. Or the dream we have to make the kind of difference that changes thousands of lives around the world, when in reality we're struggling to make a difference in our community and love people well in our own neighborhood. I don't think this means we need to give up on our dreams and desires, but I do believe we will struggle and wrestle with satisfaction in our lives unless our dreams and desires align with God's dreams and desires for us. God's call on our lives brings those dreams and desires alive in ways that we cannot fabricate or make happen on our own. Consider how Jonathan's call was connected to the dreams of his heart. That's why his armor-bearer said, "Do all that is in your heart," because he saw that Jonathan's desire to be responsible and do something about the situation was deeply connected to his heart. Consider how your dreams and desires align with God's call on your life as you answer these questions:

1. Think back to your earliest dreams as a child. What did you dream about?

2. Awakening to our dreams and desires is often the starting point for the ongoing dreaming of our call. Name a time in the past when God awakened something in you—*what were the circumstances, how did it happen, what did it mean for you, what was stirring in you, what kind of action or awareness or dreaming followed your awakening?*

3. Consider your answer to the first group discussion question, "How are you actively engaging in the dreams God has placed on your heart?" Is there anything else you would add? Or are there new dreams God has placed on your heart since you first answered this question?

4. What circumstances or situations have affected your dreams in the past or what keeps you from dreaming today?

5. **Read Matthew 11:25–26; Matthew 19:13–15; and Mark 10:13–16.** Dreaming can seem so childish for some of us, and yet notice how Jesus prioritized the presence and perspective of

children. How do these passages shape the way you think about dreaming with a childlike perspective?

6. Banning reminds us that dreaming comes from a heart-awakening with God, not an intellectual-awakening (*The Three-Mile Walk*, page 16). Perhaps this is why Jonathan's armor-bearer says, "Do all that is in your heart." And yet we are culturally conditioned to trust our minds over our hearts. How is this a struggle for you?

7. The call of God on your life is impossible without God. How do you stay connected to God and connected to moments when God is inviting you to dream about the call on your life?

8. **Read Ephesians 3:14–21.** What reasons does this passage give us to trust God with our dreams, with *his* dreams for us?

Reread Ephesians 3:20–21. Let this be your benediction as you close your time in prayer today, knowing that God can do immeasurably more than all we ask or imagine. Thank God for stirring your heart, awakening your mind, and giving you dreams beyond yourself. Ask God to help you pay attention to the desires he gives you and the opportunities he provides for you to continue dreaming as you move forward and lay claim on God's call for your life.

DAY 3: COUNTING THE COST

Here's the deal: dreams can be wildly inspiring, and yet they can also be uncomfortable, exhausting, scary, even painful at times. And most of us pay some sort of price to pursue our dreams and engage God's call on our life. But the danger isn't in the pain or the price we pay; the danger is that we will stop dreaming and stop taking risks, therefore missing out on fulfilling the dreams and desires God has for us. That's why it's important to understand what it looks like to be obedient to God's call as we pursue our dreams. When we are obedient to God's call, we know that disappointment, disillusionment, and failure are all part of the process, but that doesn't mean we give up and abandon our call. It means we lean into God as we press into our call. It means we need to keep our hopes up. Because of Jesus we have hope in *who* God says he is and *what* God says he will do. And because of Jesus, we have hope in who God says *we* are and what God is asking *us* to do. This means God's identity and mission are deeply connected to our identity and mission. In fact, they are inseparable when we're walking in obedience with God. We can count the cost and be confident in the cost because we have hope in the Resurrected Jesus. Consider what it means to count the cost of your dreams with hope as you answer these questions:

1. What price have you had to pay to pursue your dreams and the call God has placed on your heart?

2. How has disappointment, disillusionment, or failure derailed your dreams?

3. **Read Luke 14:25–33.** According to this passage, what did it cost the disciples to follow Jesus?

4. What does it look like for you to count the cost of pursuing your God-given dreams and desires? What will you have to let go of or leave behind to keep moving forward?

5. What is giving you hope on your three-mile walk with God right now as you count the cost of God's dreams and desires for you?

6. **Read 1 Peter 1:3–9.** According to this passage, what reasons do you have to place your faith and your hope in Jesus?

7. Is hope an easy or hard concept for you? Why?

8. Where do you need more hope in your life right now? How can Jesus provide the hope you need?

Read Romans 5:1–5. May you find comfort in these verses knowing that the cost you pay to pursue God's call will eventually bring peace and hope. Close your time in prayer today by thanking God for the gift of the peace and hope he gives you alongside his dreams and desires for you. Ask God to give you the perseverance and determination to keep moving forward until you experience that hope.

DAY 4: MOVING FORWARD

When Jonathan looked out at the Israelite soldiers huddling in fear and his father, Saul, sitting under the pomegranate tree refusing to act, it *provoked* him. And he did what a true soldier of Israel would do—run into the battle. Jonathan knew there was more to do than what he saw his father doing—which was nothing. Here's what we can learn from Jonathan in that moment: the call of God on our lives should provoke something inside of us that causes us to refuse to settle for anything less than all God has called us to be and to do. And if it doesn't provoke us to keep moving forward, then tragically, we settle for less than God's call and purpose for our lives. It's important to understand that when we settle for less, we're not just settling for less in our own lives, but we're causing others to miss out on the "more" God has for them too. At the very core of our Christian faith is a real, dynamic interactive relationship with God that transforms us from the inside out. And when we live out of that interactive relationship, we operate with the *mind* of Jesus the Christ, the *heart* of God the Father, and we live out the *fruit* of the Holy Spirit. We live from a whole and healthy heart. And the world needs our whole and healthy heart to provoke and inspire fellow Christians to live out of their own whole and healthy hearts. So, don't settle for less than the life God is calling you to as you keep moving forward this week.

——

Read Galatians 5. Let this be your personal reflection this week. As you meditate on this passage, use the space below to journal any thoughts, prayers, or ideas that come to mind. It might be helpful to list the fruit of the Spirit, paying attention to where they already appear in your life, or where you have room for growth as you awaken to and move toward God's call on your life.

FOR NEXT WEEK

Review the Introduction and chapters 1–2 in *The Three-Mile Walk* and use the space below to write any insights or questions from your personal study that you want to discuss at the next group meeting. In preparation for next week, read chapters 3–4 in *The Three-Mile Walk*.

—

CALL TO HOLINESS

HOW LITTLE PEOPLE KNOW WHO
THINK THAT HOLINESS IS DULL.
WHEN ONE MEETS THE REAL
THING . . . IT IS IRRESISTIBLE.
IF EVEN 10 PERCENT OF THE
WORLD'S POPULATION HAD IT,
WOULD NOT THE WHOLE WORLD
BE CONVERTED AND HAPPY?

—C. S. Lewis

WELCOME

Throughout Scripture we see a pattern of invitation and response. Every move of God begins with God pursuing individuals and inviting them into partnership to accomplish his plans and his purposes in the earth. We see this in the Creation Story with Adam and Eve (Genesis 1–2), in the burning bush with Moses (Exodus 2), with the prophet Elisha (2 Kings 9), all the way into the New Testament where we see Jesus call his first disciples (Matthew 4), and the invitation of the Holy Spirit given to the early believers (Acts 1–2). Even in the last pages of Scripture, we find this pattern of invitation and response when Jesus announced, "Behold, I stand at the door and knock. If anyone hears my voice and opens the door, I will come in to him and dine with him, and he with me" (Revelation 3:20 NKJV).

We find this same pattern throughout church history too. Every awakening, revival, outpouring of the Spirit, or move of God is connected to individuals who have responded to the call of God. God's invitation to us is not always loud or obvious, but the invitation is *always* there. And our response to the invitation is what starts our *three-mile walk* with God.

The first leg of our journey on the *three-mile walk* is the call to holiness. As an image-bearer of God, God calls us to be holy because he is holy. But living a life of holiness isn't the key to getting God's attention. Living a life of holiness is actually our response to God's invitation. It's a byproduct of our "yes" to God's call on our lives, our "yes" to living out the dreams and desires God has for each one of us. And yet sometimes we're held back by our own fears—our fear of failure and our fear of rejection. This holding back happens in moments when we are crippled by indecision, or when we feel stuck, or when we're unable or unwilling to move forward. We often ask ourselves, "But what if I mess up?" We want to avoid these painful experiences at all costs, and we become paralyzed by fear—afraid to say no to God's call, and yet deeply afraid to say yes. When we allow these fears of failure and rejection to keep us from moving forward, it's as if we're saying failure is more powerful than God. And we're okay to be sidelined on our journey.

We *must* believe God is greater than our failures if we are to keep moving forward. That's why the apostle Paul reminds us in Romans 8 that we are *more than conquerors*: "What then, shall we say in response to these things? If God is for us, who can be against us?" (verse 31). This is my prayer for you—for us—as we move forward on this *three-mile walk*; that we would willingly trust God with our failures and our successes, knowing he is *for us* and *with us* when we say yes to God's invitation to live the life he's called us to live.

SHARE

If you or any of your group members are just meeting for the first time, take a few minutes to introduce yourselves and share any insights you have from last week's personal study. Next, to kick things off for the group time, discuss one of the following questions:

- When have your fears held you back from saying yes to God?
  — *or* —
- Describe someone whom exemplifies the idea of *holiness* from your perspective.

READ

Invite someone to read aloud the following passage. Listen for fresh insight as you continue reading the story of Jonathan in 1 Samuel 14, and then share any new thoughts with the group through the questions that follow.

Jonathan said, "Come on, then; we will cross over toward them and let them see us. If they say to us, 'Wait there until we come to you,' we will stay where we are and not go up to them. But if they say, 'Come up to us,' we will climb up, because that will be our sign that the LORD has given them into our hands." So both of them showed themselves to the Philistine outpost. "Look!" said the Philistines. "The Hebrews are crawling out of the holes they were hiding in." The men of the outpost shouted to Jonathan and his armor-bearer, "Come up to us and we'll teach you a lesson." So Jonathan said to his armor-bearer, "Climb up after me; the LORD has given them into the hand of Israel." Jonathan climbed up, using his hands and feet, with his armor-bearer right behind him. The Philistines fell before Jonathan, and his armor-bearer followed and killed behind him. In that first attack Jonathan and his armor-bearer killed some twenty men in an area of about half an acre. Then panic struck the whole army—those in the camp and field, and those in the outposts and raiding parties—and the ground shook. It was a panic sent by God. Saul's lookouts at Gibeah in Benjamin saw the army melting away in all directions. Then Saul said to the men who were with him, "Muster the forces and see who has left us." When they did, it was Jonathan and his armor-bearer who were not there. Saul said to Ahijah, "Bring the ark of God." (At that time it was with the Israelites.) While Saul was talking to the priest, the tumult in the Philistine camp increased more and more. So Saul said to the priest, "Withdraw your hand." Then Saul and all his men assembled and went to the battle. They found the Philistines in total confusion, striking each other with their swords. Those Hebrews who had previously been with the Philistines and had gone up with them to their camp went over to the

Israelites who were with Saul and Jonathan. When all the Israelites who had hidden in the hill country of Ephraim heard that the Philistines were on the run, they joined the battle in hot pursuit. So on that day the LORD saved Israel, and the battle moved on beyond Beth Aven. (1 Samuel 14:8–23).

What is one key insight that stands out to you from this passage?

If you were Jonathan, what would you be thinking or feeling about Saul's indecision in the moment of battle? What is so significant about Jonathan's armor-bearer in this story?

WATCH

Play the video for session two. As you and your group watch, use the following outline to record any thoughts or key points that stand out to you.

Notes

The First Mile: Holiness

Is it just a list of do's and don'ts?

"I am the LORD, who brought you up out of Egypt to be your God; therefore be holy, because I am holy." (Leviticus 11:45)

Repenting of sins.
Setting yourself apart.

Jonathan's Example of Holiness

He has to separate from things and set himself apart for God.

The Parable of the Wedding Banquet (Matthew 22)

The journey starts with an invitation: God is awakening your heart and stirring you.

"For many are called, but few are chosen." (Matthew 22:14 NKJV)

Few respond to the invitation.

———

Every believer has a call on their life.
The Invitation: one big YES.

Holiness Is 100 Percent

Holiness is relational.
The motivation for holiness is our love for God.

"Therefore, having these promises, beloved, let us cleanse ourselves from all filthiness of the flesh and spirit, perfecting holiness in the fear of God." (2 Corinthians 7:1 NKJV)

God's desire for us to be holy comes from his desire to connect with us as sons and daughters.

The Help of the Holy Spirit

Justification: the one-time legal act when you got saved.
Sanctification: the everyday work of the Holy Spirit in your life after you've been saved.

"And we all, who with unveiled faces contemplate the Lord's glory, are being transformed into his image with ever-increasing glory, which comes from the Lord, who is the Spirit." (2 Corinthians 3:18)

The first mile of holiness is about surrendering to our relationship with God.

DISCUSS

Take a few minutes with your group members to discuss what you just watched and explore these concepts together.

1. How would you describe *holiness* as a result of what you learned today? How do Jonathan and his armor-bearer exemplify *holiness* in 1 Samuel 14?

2. How is this different or similar to the way you would have described *holiness* based on *your* past experience of God, or *holiness* as described by your church community?

3. **Read Mark 12:28–34.** In what tangible ways are you loving God with all of your heart, mind, and strength? How would the people around you answer this question *for* you?

4. *Holiness* almost always involves *surrender*. What does *surrender* mean to you, and how are you *surrendering* to God right now?

5. Before Jonathan could fully surrender, he had to separate from anything holding him back from pursuing God's call. What do you need to separate from so you can more fully pursue *holiness* and *surrender* to God?

6. **Read 2 Corinthians 3.** How does the Spirit help us live a life of *holiness*? What does *holiness* look like for you as a group or as a faith community?

RESPOND

Briefly review the outline for the video teaching and any notes you took. In the space below, write down the most significant point you took away from this session.

Is there a specific action step you can take this week, as an individual and as a community, to say yes to God's invitation to walk in *holiness*?

PRAY

End the gathering by praying with your group and, if you are comfortable in doing so, briefly share one area or one way you will surrender to God this week as you pursue God's holiness for your life. Pray that God would clearly show you what you need to surrender and give you courage to separate yourself from whatever is holding you back so you can say yes to God as you pursue God's holiness. Write down any specific requests in the space below so you can remember to continue praying throughout the week.

2

SESSION

This week spend some time with God each day to explore this topic in the Bible as you engage in any or all of the following activities. Be sure to read the reflection questions and make a few notes that you can share at the next group meeting.

DAY 1: THE INVITATION

I think it's really important for us to understand God's heart toward us. God never puts demands on us to love him or follow him. In fact, it's the exact opposite. Throughout Scripture we see God inviting the Israelites and the early followers of Jesus—and now us—into a deep, rich, and meaningful life; a life of human flourishing. Even when we read one of God's commands in Scripture, like the Greatest Commandment in Matthew 22, those commands are always for our protection and our well-being. It's important to understand that the call to holiness isn't a command or a demand; it's an *invitation*. The invitation is God's call on your life, and it looks like God awakening your heart and stirring something inside of you. And the *three-mile walk* starts with this invitation. However, like most invitations and RSVPs, a response is required. That's why Jesus says, "Many are called, but few are chosen" not just once but *twice* in the New Testament. It's not about God choosing us; it's about us choosing God. It's about us saying yes to God's invitation to live out the calling God has placed on our lives. So, take a few moments to consider your response to God's invitation as you answer these questions:

1. **Read Matthew 20:1–16 in the NKJV translation.** What stands out to you in this passage? What seems to be the teachable lesson in this parable told by Jesus?

2. **Read Matthew 22:1–14 in the NIV or NKJV translations.** What stands out to you in this passage? What seems to be the teachable lesson in this parable told by Jesus?

3. What invitation is God extending to you right now as you consider your *three-mile walk* with him?

4. Often, one big invitation also opens the door to a few smaller invitations. How has this been true for you? Are there small invitations that have come with God's main invitation for you in this

season of life? *i.e., a friend of mine once sensed God's invitation for her was to WAIT for God. In the midst of her waiting season, God clearly provided opportunities for her to write, teach, and contribute to her community in profound ways that had not been available to her before the season of waiting.*

5. Are there invitations still waiting for your response? Or invitations you've turned down that you now wish you would have said yes to? If so, ask God to redeem those invitations in whatever way God sees best.

6. How have you been inspired by the people around you who have said yes to God's invitation and call on their lives?

7. What can you learn from those people or their situations?

8. **Read Revelation 3:20.** What is at stake if you say no to God's invitation to you? Be specific with your answer.

Read John 12:16. It's not always easy to understand God's invitation in our lives. Even the disciples struggled to understand the words and purpose of Jesus at times. And yet, the disciples knew they could trust the nature and the character of Jesus based on their experience of him, and they could trust God as he revealed himself through Jesus. May that be your prayer today—that you grow in your understanding of God's invitation to you, and that you have a deeper sense of trust in God as he revealed himself through Jesus and as he continues to reveal himself to you in your everyday life.

DAY 2: HOLINESS

If you're going to embrace a lifestyle of holiness, it's important that you begin to understand what *holiness* really means. It's a concept we often sing about in worship songs, and yet most of us find it challenging to accurately describe *holiness*. The good thing is, we're not alone. The writers of the New Testament wrestled with how to define holiness in the days and years following the death and resurrection of Jesus. However, they found comfort in knowing they were not alone. Without the physical presence of Jesus, the early Christians had the Holy Spirit as their guide. And so do we. There will be times when we wrestle with the concept of *holiness* in our lives. We ask, how do we live it, how do we describe it, how do we measure it so we know if we're making progress and moving forward? These are valid questions we often hear in the church. And while we may not always have clarity, we do have the Holy Spirit as our guide, and we have the Bible to give us words to help define *holiness*. Consider what it looks like for you to pursue *holiness* with the help of the Holy Spirit—just as the early church did—as you answer these questions:

1. **Reread 1 Samuel 14:8–23.** Now that you've had some time

to consider *holiness* in light of Jonathan's example and your group discussion time, what words, images, or examples would you use to describe *holiness*?

2. **Read 2 Corinthians 7.** According to the apostle Paul, the author of this letter to the Corinthians, *holiness* is an outgrowth of repentance. What other characteristics are a byproduct of *holiness* and repentance (verses 9–11)?

3. Do you see repentance as a necessary part of *holiness*? Why or why not?

4. **Read 1 Peter 1:13–25.** What characteristics are connected to the idea of *holiness* in this passage?

5. Consider your own pursuit of *holiness* as it relates to 1 Peter. How are you exercising obedience, fearful reverence, and belief in God as you love one another?

6. Are there other examples of *holiness* from the Bible that inspire you on your own journey? If so, how do those examples encourage you to live a holy life?

7. How are you leaning on the Holy Spirit as your guide in life and in your pursuit of *holiness*?

8. What steps toward *holiness* do you need to take today or this week? Be specific with an action step and a date by which you will have taken or completed that step. Share your action step(s) with a trusted friend or mentor for accountability.

Read 2 Timothy 1:8–9. The aim of our *holiness* isn't for our own sake but for the sake of God. That's why God has called us with a holy calling—for his own purpose. Thank God that your pursuit of *holiness* is ultimately in his hands. And ask God to give you the strength and foresight to accept his invitation so you may be obedient to his call on your life as you pursue *holiness*. May you also be aware of opportunities to encourage others in their pursuit of *holiness* on this *three-mile* journey.

DAY 3: SEPARATION

There's been a lot of conversation in the church over what it means to be "separated" as followers of Jesus. This idea has been addressed by the brightest minds and greatest theologians for centuries. I don't want to be overly simplistic about what it means to be separated, and yet I think there are very clear answers and examples in Scripture as to how this idea of separation relates to God's call on our lives. Here's my take on this idea of separation: every believer has the call of God on their life, and what separates us isn't the idea that we either believe or do not believe; what separates us is how we respond to the invitation of God's call on our lives. There will be some of us who say no, others who ignore the call, and others who say yes. From my perspective, ignoring or not responding to God's call is still a response. It's a response that communicates no without actually saying no to God. So, the separation we are talking about isn't between Christians and non-Christians; it's between those who respond yes or no to God's invitation. A life of separation is being willing to say yes to God's call, being willing to pursue holiness, and surrendering 100 percent of who we are to God in the midst of following that call—even when those around us choose not to do the same. Our motivation for this kind of separation—our big "yes" to God—is our love for God. Your love for God is the motivation for your response to God's invitation, your pursuit of holiness, your separation, and your surrender. Reflect on the idea of separation as you consider your answers to these questions:

1. **Read Leviticus 20:22–26.** How does God separate the Israelites from the rest of the people in the land? Why?

2. How have you experienced separation as a result of your "yes" to God?

3. Is there someone in your life who models this well, someone who has embraced some sort of separation as a result of God's call on their lives?

4. At times, saying yes to God creates separation in our lives from those who are not following God's call. How have you experienced disruption or disconnection in your relationships or in your life as a result of your obedience to God's call?

5. **Read Leviticus 19:33–34.** God reminds the Israelites to love others and treat them well. What do you do to love people and treat them well even when you feel separated from them by your response to God's call on your life?

6. Consider your answer to question 3. How does this person love others well while living a separated life?

7. **Read Deuteronomy 6.** Why do you think Moses needed to give these commands to the Israelites as they were about to cross over the Jordan River into the promised land, after all that God had already done for them?

8. How does loving God motivate you to say yes to God's invitation to walk in holiness, separation, and surrender?

Read Mark 12:28–34. Jesus reminds his followers of the Greatest Commandment and, in doing so, he also redefines the law for his Jewish followers. He communicates the idea that loving God is more important than all the burnt offerings, sacrifices, and additional commandments required by Jewish law up until that point. So, the next time you get wrapped up in your best attempts to be righteous and live a life of holiness, remember that loving God, loving others, and loving yourself supersedes living a perfect life. Loving God is what separates you from others, and it's what allows you to say yes to God's invitation to live out his call on your life. Ask God to let your love for him be your highest goal as you continue on your *three-mile walk.*

DAY 4: SURRENDER

When Jonathan and his armor-bearer left to head out on their three-mile walk through the Valley of Mikmash (also spelled

Michmash), they left their safety net behind. Meaning, they left behind their food, their beds, their company, and the security of a crowd. They had no certainty of success. But they did it for one reason—because they trusted God. They also knew that God needed a few soldiers in that moment who were willing to put their lives entirely in his hands. That's why we hear Jonathan say, "Perhaps the LORD will act in our behalf. Nothing can hinder the LORD from saving, whether by many or by few" (1 Samuel 14:6). They kept moving forward and didn't stop until God showed up. They surrendered their ideas, their strategies, and their plans to God's call on their lives in that moment. I don't know about you, but that's the way I want to live my life—fully surrendered to God. And just in case you're curious, I think surrender often looks like saying:

"Yes, Jesus, I will follow you."

"Yes, I will be a leader in my generation."

"Yes, I will be a good parent and a godly partner to my spouse."

"Yes, I will stand for the truth of God's kingdom."

"Yes, I will contribute my voice and my strengths to change the world."

"Yes, I will serve others and surrender my life out of love to you, God."

"Yes, I will work to see God's purposes fulfilled in the earth."

This is surrender.

———

Read John 14:15–31. Let this be your personal reflection this week. May you understand that surrender flows out of your love for

God and that you're not alone in your surrendering. As you meditate on this passage, use the space below to journal any thoughts, prayers, or ideas that come to mind.

FOR NEXT WEEK

Use the space below to write any key insights or questions from your personal study that you want to discuss at the next group meeting. In preparation for next week, review chapters 5–7 in *The Three-Mile Walk*.

—

CALL TO COURAGE

DON'T PUT A PERIOD WHERE

GOD HAS PUT A COMMA.

Charles Crabtree

WELCOME

One of the reasons I'm so passionate about encouraging other people is because engaging the call of God on our lives requires courage. You will not become who God has called you to be or get where God has called you to go apart from courage. It took a massive amount of courage for Jonathan to engage God's call on his life and start out on his three-mile journey. I think that's why he knew he needed the encouragement of someone else on the journey—his armor-bearer. The courage we need on the three-mile walk isn't primarily the courage to make grand leaps of faith or take huge risks. It's primarily the courage to keep moving forward—to keep putting one foot in front of the other, to keep walking from one mile to the next, even when the journey is more challenging than we expected.

We need courage to do the work of navigating our journey because the terrain is often hard, and we *will* get discouraged at some point along the way. We will make mistakes, discover painful blind spots, feel weak and unprepared, or become frustrated and lost. We will wonder if we have enough strength or energy to finish the journey and fulfill God's call. But when we walk with courage, we know the discouragement we face does not mean the end of our story or the end of our journey.

Most of us don't need more teaching or tools to step into our call with courage. We just need to choose to do it. Either you're going to live with courage or not. So, what does it look like to walk with courage? I think we can take a cue from the life of Jonathan, who kept his eyes fixed on God. Just like Jonathan and his armor-bearer, we move forward with courage when we move forward with God by acknowledging his presence and the instructions found in his Word. And we move forward with greater courage when we are willing to walk in community.

No matter where you find yourself on your *three-mile walk* today, I believe God is inviting you to stand up, dust yourself off from discouragement, and move forward with courage. And you can take courage because God is with you in Spirit, in Word, and within the community of one another. As you move into group discussion, consider the courageous steps you need to take today to keep walking with God. And if you're already moving forward with courage, then consider how you can inspire courage in someone around you. Look for someone who needs to be reminded of God's presence, God's promises, and God's love through you as you move forward together on the *three-mile walk* with courage.

SHARE

Begin your group time by inviting anyone to share his or her insights from last week's personal study. Next, to kick things off, discuss one of the following questions:

- When was the last time you felt discouraged, and why?
— *or* —
- What does courage look like, feel like, or sound like to you?

READ

Invite someone to read aloud the following passage regarding Elijah. It's important to understand this snapshot of Elijah's life happens *after* God shows up in some amazing ways in Elijah's life, even causing the nation of Israel to turn back to God. Listen for fresh insight and then share any new thoughts with the group through the questions that follow.

Now Ahab told Jezebel everything Elijah had done and how he had killed all the prophets with the sword. So Jezebel sent a messenger to Elijah to say, "May the gods deal with me, be it ever so severely, if by this time tomorrow I do not make your life like that of one of them." Elijah was afraid and ran for his life. When he came to Beersheba in Judah, he left his servant there, while he himself went a day's journey into the wilderness. He came to a broom bush, sat down under it and prayed that he might die. "I have had enough, LORD," he said. "Take my life, I am no better than my ancestors." Then he lay down under the bush and fell asleep. All at once an angel touched him and said, "Get up and eat." He looked around, and there by his head was some bread baked over hot coals, and a jar of water. He ate and drank and then lay down again. The angel of the LORD came back a second time and touched him and said, "Get up and eat, for the journey is too much for you." So he got up and ate and drank. Strengthened by that food, he traveled forty days and forty nights until he reached Horeb, the mountain of God. There he went into a cave and spent the night. And the word of the LORD came to him: "What are you doing here, Elijah?" He replied, "I have been very zealous for the LORD God Almighty. The Israelites have rejected your covenant, torn down your altars, and put your prophets to death with the sword. I am the only one left, and now they are trying to kill me too. (1 Kings 19:1–10).

What is one key insight that stands out to you from this passage?

How did Elijah respond to the discouragement he was feeling?

WATCH

Play the video for session three. As you and your group watch, use the following outline to record any thoughts or key points that stand out to you.

Notes

The Second Mile on the Three-Mile Walk *Is Courage*

> "Do all that is in your heart. Go then; here I am with you, according to your heart." (1 Samuel 14:7 NKJV)

Discouragement, lies, and the story of Elijah.

———

The three lies of discouragement:

    1. God is not with us.

    2. The situation is hopeless.

    3. We are all alone.

The Key Question: How Do We Stay Encouraged?

The three ways God gives us courage:

    1. The presence of God

"Wait on the LORD; be of good courage, and he shall strengthen your heart; wait, I say, on the LORD!" (Psalm 27:14 NKJV)

2. God's Word

"Jesus answered, 'It is written: "Man shall not live on bread alone, but on every word that comes from the mouth of God."'" (Matthew 4:4)

———

"...For he himself has said, 'I will never leave you nor forsake you.' So we may boldly say: The Lord is my helper; I will not fear. What can man do to me?" (Hebrews 13:5-6 NKJV)

3. Family and Community

"I long to see you so that I may impart to you some spiritual gift to make you strong—that is, that you and I may be mutually encouraged by each other's faith." (Romans 1:11-12)

The Pattern of Community in Scripture

- Moses and Joshua
- Mordecai and Esther
- Barnabas and Paul
- Paul and Timothy

Discouragement is part of the journey. Keep living a life of courage.

DISCUSS

Take a few minutes with your group members to discuss what you just watched and explore these concepts together.

1. What does courage mean to you? Share about something courageous that happened in your own life.

2. Consider the community around you. Who exemplifies this idea of walking in courage on the journey of following God's call, and why?

3. How can you identify with the story of Elijah? In what areas of life have you experienced the most discouragement: feeling like God had abandoned you, like the situation was hopeless, or like you were all alone?

4. **Read Joshua 1.** Notice how many times the Lord encouraged Joshua to be courageous because God was with Joshua. How does the presence of God instill a sense of courage within you?

5. How does the Word of God, the Bible, give you courage?

6. **Read Deuteronomy 31:1–8.** Not only did Moses encourage Joshua and remind Joshua of God's presence with him, he did it in front of their community—the entire nation of Israel. How has your community encouraged you? And how have you contributed to the encouraging support for someone else?

RESPOND

Briefly review the outline for the video teaching and any notes you took. In the space below, write down the most significant point you took away from this session.

Is there a specific action step you can take this week to move toward living a life of calling *and* courage?

PRAY

End the gathering by praying for each other. Pray especially that God would help you move forward with courage and embrace discouragement as a natural part of the journey. May God help you remember God's presence, God's Word, and the community God has placed around you. Write down any specific requests in the space below so you can remember to continue praying throughout the week.

3

Remember King Saul who sat discouraged and powerless under the pomegranate tree believing that God had abandoned him, that his situation was hopeless, and that he was all alone? Jonathan was in the same predicament as his father, and yet did not respond the same way as King Saul. Why do you think two people from the same bloodline in the same situation responded in two completely different ways? I'm sure there are a lot of factors, including personality, and yet what seems to set Jonathan and Saul apart here in this moment is *courage*. Jonathan responded with courage in his heart—and with a plan. And he had a courageous friend who acknowledged Jonathan's own courageous plan by saying, "Do all that is in your heart . . ." (1 Samuel 14:7 NKJV). Here's what I want you to consider this week: God never promised that our journey would be easy, but God did promise to always be with us on the journey. Life will be hard at times—with or without God. But we can make it through those hard times with courage if we're willing to trust God.

DAY 1: DISCOURAGEMENT

It's discouraging when things don't work out the way we thought—when we lose a business, when a marriage fails, when illness strikes, when church doors close, when things are harder than expected. Remember the story of Elijah from 1 Kings 19? He came through a major victory, then quickly hit rock bottom with discouragement. He felt like God had abandoned him, the situation was hopeless, and he was all alone. But when we read his story, we realize none of those feelings were actually true. They were all lies he believed—lies from the enemy.

The enemy's primary objective has always been to discourage us with lies because he knows we can't fulfill the call of God on our life without courage. He knows we get easily sidetracked by discouragement, so if he can't discourage us from *starting* the journey, he will be sure to discourage us while we're *on* the journey. This is important to understand because so many of us are discouraged by the fact that we're even facing discouragement while pursuing God's call.

If discouragement is holding you back, I want you to know you already have enough talent, training, skills, and information to move forward, but you need to rise above your discouragement, guard your heart in the process, and step forward into God's call *with courage.* Discouragement along the journey is a given. But it's up to us how we deal with this discouragement on our journey. You need to name your discouragement so you can move forward with courage. Consider your own discouragement as you answer these questions:

1. What kind of discouragement are you facing right now? Anything

similar to Elijah's story and his feelings of abandonment from God, hopelessness, or isolation?

2. How has that discouragement affected your three-mile walk with God?

3. **Read John 8:44 and John 10:10.** Is there a pattern or obvious way the enemy tries to discourage you from God's call on your life?

4. **Read 2 Corinthians 2:11 in the NASB translation.** How do you stay alert to the enemy's schemes in your life?

5. **Read John 8:31–38.** How does Jesus encourage his early followers to combat the lies of the enemy? How does this passage encourage you as well?

6. In *The Three-Mile Walk,* Banning provides three keys to combating discouragement (chapter 6): key one—the power of a meal and a nap; key two—the Navy Seal concept of keeping one foot in the water (or keep one foot in a place where you thrive); and key three—show up with someone else. Which one of these keys do you need to put into practice this week as you lean into your discouragement?

7. Discouragement is an experience we cannot avoid—it's an experience we must learn to walk through and become resilient in the process. How has your discouragement taught you to be resilient—to withstand and recover from difficult circumstances?

8. How has God used your past discouragement to allow you to encourage others?

Read James 5:7–20. You may be in the middle of a really discouraging season or a difficult leg of your three-mile journey, but you will endure! And may you take comfort in the reminder that "Elijah was a man with a nature like ours" (verse 17 NKJV). Ask God to show you what lies you've been believing in the midst of your discouragement and to help you replace them with his truth. Close today by thanking God for giving you the opportunity to learn from your discouragement as you grow in your resilience and your awareness of God *because of* your discouragement, not *in spite of* your discouragement.

DAY 2: TAKE COURAGE IN GOD'S PRESENCE

Throughout the Israelites' journey from Egypt through the desert and into the promised land, we hear God reminding the Israelites of his presence over and over again—especially as we read Exodus, Leviticus, Deuteronomy, and Joshua. While this might sound like overkill for the Israelites, the truth is, they needed the constant reminder of God's presence because they were consistently forgetting about his presence. Sound familiar? I can't even begin to tell you how many times I've tried to do life on my own because I wasn't aware of God's presence. I was either too preoccupied to include God in my plans, or I had convinced myself that God just didn't care. But living with courage requires acknowledging God's presence in our lives *at all times.* And we can trust God's presence from the moment he told the Israelites he would never leave them or forsake them (Deuteronomy 31) to the moment when Jesus physically arrived on Earth to be with us (Luke 2) to the moment he gave us the Holy Spirit as our guide (Acts 2). And then, even when we're aware of God's presence, there is still the choice we have to make to embrace God's presence. This is truly what it means to live with courage—to acknowledge and embrace God's presence in our lives.

So, the next time we're faced with doubt, discouragement, and delay, we must ask ourselves, *Will we trust ourselves or will we trust the presence of God?* And when God seems slow to respond, we must ask, *Will we question his character and his heart toward us or will we trust his presence?* God allows doubt, discouragement, and delay so we learn to trust his presence in our lives. And trusting God's presence in our lives leads to patient endurance and contented confidence. These are the traits needed if we're going to not only thrive on the *three-mile walk* but experience the fullness of our relationship with God. Consider how you are walking with courage in the presence of God as you answer these questions:

1. Truth be told, we've all struggled to acknowledge or embrace God's presence at times. What makes it hard for you to trust God's presence in your life now or in past seasons when doubt, delay, and discouragement invaded?

2. **Read Romans 5:13.** According to this passage, what is the result of trusting God's presence in our lives? Why does this matter for you?

3. How have you sensed God's presence in your life lately?

4. How has God's presence given you courage?

5. **Read James 1:4.** How does this passage reflect patient endurance, one of the key elements of living with courage by trusting God's presence?

6. **Read Philippians 4:11–13.** How does this passage reflect contented confidence—another key element of living with courage by trusting in God's presence?

7. What do you think will happen if you attempt to live with courage *without* the presence of God? Do you have a past experience or example of this?

8. What step(s) will you take this week to be actively mindful of God's presence as you continue living out your call with courage?

Read Jeremiah 29:11. So much of our awareness of God's presence requires *trust*. And for some of us, our life experiences have made *trust* a tricky thing. Ask God to show you what it's like to trust the presence of God and his plans for you so you can live with courage and experience all of God's dreams and desires for you.

DAY 3: TAKE COURAGE IN GOD'S WORD

If we can take courage and trust in God's presence, then we can take courage and trust in God's Word too. For many early followers of Jesus, God's presence and the Word of God were synonymous because of these words from the apostle John: *In the beginning the Word was God* (John 1:1) and *the Word became flesh* (John 1:14).

God was, and is, God's Word. There are a lot of theological layers here. But what I want you to hear is that you can trust God's Word, meaning the Bible, because of the revelation of God in the Word— because of the way God's Word reveals God's nature, his character, and his heart toward us. And we can trust the way the Bible points to Jesus as the living Word. The Bible says we are not to live on bread alone but by every word that proceeds from the mouth of God (Matthew 4:4). God's words actually become fuel for us—for our *three-mile walk*.

1. Have you ever read a Bible verse (or passage) and it was *exactly* what you needed to hear in that moment? What was the verse and the situation?

2. Have you ever been inspired or felt prompted to share a verse or passage with a friend, or even a stranger, and it was exactly what *they* needed? What were the circumstances?

3. **Read Deuteronomy 8:1–5 and Matthew 4:4.** According to these passages, what is the meaning of the phrase, "Man shall not live by bread alone"?

4. How do you stay connected to God's Word on your *three-mile walk*? What practices or disciplines have been helpful to your understanding of God's Word?

5. **Read Proverbs 4:20–23.** How are you keeping God's words in your sight and within your heart on the journey?

6. Why is it important to guard your heart with the Word of God as you move forward with courage?

7. **Read John 1:1–18.** What stands out to you about this passage? How does this passage encourage or strengthen your understanding of God's Word?

8. How would you respond to the friend who says, "Is it really *that* important to read the Bible?" Can you think of a helpful way to respond by sharing how God's Word has made a difference for you, particularly as you live out God's call in your life?

Read Ephesians 1:17–23. May this be your prayer today: that God would give you the Spirit of wisdom and revelation as you *read* God's Word, and as you *experience* God's Word through your understanding of Jesus and your relationship with the Holy Spirit. This is essential to moving forward with courage as you live out God's dreams and desires for you. Thank God that he has made a way to be with you in Word, in flesh, and in Spirit.

DAY 4: TAKE COURAGE IN COMMUNITY

I'm convinced there is a depth of courage found *only* in community—in being surrounded with people who believe in you and challenge you. When we distance or isolate ourselves from people and believe the lie that we are all alone, we are separating ourselves from the very encouragement God is trying to release in us, so we can be all he has called us to be and do all he has called us to do. God puts people in your life to run with you.

Remember the story I shared about my dad running the San Francisco marathon? God puts other "runners" or sojourners in our lives to run alongside us through the most challenging miles of our journey. That's why the story in 1 Samuel 14 is so important. It isn't just about Jonathan—it's about Jonathan *and* his armor-bearer. Community is one of God's primary resources for helping us stay healthy and stay encouraged as we embrace God's call. But the enemy is keenly aware of the importance of our community; this is why he tries to isolate us from each other.

Think about all the times you've been struggling, or someone around you has been struggling, and the first sign of this struggle is often to withdraw from community. That's why it is so important to understand that God instills a greater depth of courage in our life when we are connected to his family and community. We need fellow "runners" who help us get from one mile-marker to the next on our journey. For this reason, God puts community around us to come and believe in us and speak courage to us. Not only do we want to receive this kind of community and live out personal lives of courage, but we want to give this kind of community by drawing out the courage of other people as well.

—

Read Hebrews 10:19–25. Let this be your personal reflection this week. May you understand that courage flows out of God's presence with you—both in spirit and in word—and out of the community God has given to you. As you meditate on this passage, use the space below to journal any thoughts, prayers, or ideas that come to mind. Make note of what stands out to you in this passage, and then write down the list of names in your community from whom you are *receiving* courage and to whom you are *giving* courage.

FOR NEXT WEEK

Use the space below to write any key insights or questions from your personal study that you want to discuss at the next group meeting. In preparation for next week, review section three (chapters 8–10) in *The Three-Mile Walk*.

—

CALL TO FAITH

HOPE IS THE SOIL THAT

FAITH GROWS IN.

Banning Liebscher

WELCOME

When my wife and I first got married, we had to work hard on our communication skills. Same when I started leading a team at church, or when my kids were old enough to reason with me, or when I started coaching basketball. In each of these areas, it took a while until everyone involved understood one another well enough to make decisions together, solve problems together, navigate conflict together, work together, and win together. It required a level of trust and faith in the faces around the table or on the court. It meant we had to understand the nature and the character of every individual involved in the conversation for us to move forward as a "team." This is a small window into God's call to faith in our lives.

Faith comes from understanding the nature and character of God. The way we express our faith is that we expect God to show up in the same way over and over again. And when God shows up in our lives, God isn't showing up to prove something to us; he's showing up to teach us who he is—a present, loving, faithful, hope-filled, peaceful, and, yes, powerful Father God. He's showing up to teach us that we can choose faith over fear and doubt in our lives because he's trustworthy. That's why I love the Psalms. They give us clear pathways for finding God and following God so we can move from fear and doubt to faith. But making that move from fear to faith isn't always easy.

I often wonder if Jonathan was able to move forward with faith and courage because he saw King Saul doing the exact opposite—sitting passively under a tree, tethered to his fear and doubt and struggling to respond to God in faith. Jonathan had a real-life example of what it looked like to *not* move forward in faith, and perhaps this is what propelled him to do exactly the opposite; to come up with a plan to partner with God in what God was already doing in the Valley of Mikmash (or Michmash). *And* Jonathan had a friend who was willing to move forward in faith with him. I doubt the same was true of King Saul; otherwise, this story may have gone a different way. Faith is the reason Jonathan could say, "I know who God is, I know what he can do, I know he's with me, and I know if I step out with him in this moment, he's going to be there with me" (1 Samuel 14:6, paraphrased). And faith is the reason we can respond the same way to God today.

The *three-mile walk* is a walk of faith from start to end. It's a walk that requires us to move forward into the unknown and the unseen as we engage God's call in our lives. As we move forward with the *Call to Faith,* we're diving into these crucial areas of conversation: understanding the four truths of faith, surviving faith under fire, maintaining a crucial supply line to our faith, and waiting actively in faith for God to move. Let's keep moving.

SHARE

Begin your group time by inviting anyone to share their insights from last week's personal study. Next, to kick things off, discuss one of the following questions:

- When have you done something that required a tremendous amount of faith?

  — or —

- Is there someone in your life whom you would consider a "hero of faith"? Someone who is faithful at all costs to God's call on their life?

READ

Invite someone to read aloud the following passage, often referred to as "The Hall of Faith," a play on words for The Hall of Fame. Listen for fresh insight and then share any new thoughts with the group through the questions that follow.

> By faith Abraham, when God tested him, offered Isaac as a sacrifice. He who had embraced the promises was about to sacrifice his one and only son, even though God had said to him, "It is through Isaac that your offspring will be reckoned." Abraham reasoned that God could even raise the dead, and so in a manner of speaking he did receive Isaac back from death. By faith Isaac blessed Jacob and Esau in regard to their future. By faith Jacob, when he was dying, blessed each of Joseph's sons, and worshiped as he leaned on the top of his staff. By faith Joseph, when his end was near, spoke about the exodus of the Israelites from Egypt and gave instructions concerning the burial of his bones. By faith Moses' parents hid him for three months after he was born, because they saw he was no ordinary child, and they were not afraid of the king's edict. By faith Moses, when he had grown up, refused to be known as the son of Pharaoh's daughter. He chose to be mistreated along with the people of God rather than to enjoy the fleeting pleasures of sin. He regarded disgrace for the sake of Christ as of greater value than the treasures of Egypt, because he was looking ahead to his reward. By faith he left Egypt, not fearing the king's anger; he persevered because he saw him who is invisible. By faith he kept the Passover and the application of blood, so that the destroyer of the firstborn would not touch

the firstborn of Israel. By faith the people passed through the Red Sea as on dry land; but when the Egyptians tried to do so, they were drowned. By faith the walls of Jericho fell, after the army had marched around them for seven days. By faith the prostitute Rahab, because she welcomed the spies, was not killed with those who were disobedient. And what more shall I say? I do not have time to tell about Gideon, Barak, Samson and Jephthah, about David and Samuel and the prophets, who through faith conquered kingdoms, administered justice, and gained what was promised; who shut the mouths of lions, quenched the fury of the flames, and escaped the edge of the sword; whose weakness was turned to strength; and who became powerful in battle and routed foreign armies. Women received back their dead, raised to life again. There were others who were tortured, refusing to be released so that they might gain an even better resurrection. Some faced jeers and flogging, and even chains and imprisonment. They were put to death by stoning; they were sawed in two; they were killed by the sword. They went about in sheepskins and goatskins, destitute, persecuted and mistreated—the world was not worthy of them. They wandered in deserts and mountains, living in caves and in holes in the ground. These were all commended for their faith, yet none of them received what had been promised, since God had planned something better for us so that only together with us would they be made perfect. (Hebrews 11:17–40)

What was one thing that stood out to you from the Scripture?

How do you make sense of the idea that these individuals were commended for their faith, and yet none received what had been promised?

WATCH

Play the video for session four. As you and your group watch, use the following outline to record any thoughts or key points that stand out to you.

Notes

The Third Mile of the Journey Is Faith

"For we live by faith, not by sight." (2 Corinthians 5:7)

———

"But without faith it is impossible to please him, for he who comes to God must believe that he is, and that he is a rewarder of those who diligently seek him." (Hebrews 11:6 NKJV)

———

"…and if I have a faith that can move mountains, but do not have love, I am nothing…" (1 Corinthians 13:2)

———

Jonathan's faith

> "Now faith is the substance of things hoped for, the evidence of things not seen." (Hebrews 11:1 NKJV)

Biblical Hope

A healthy heart: Hope comes from a healthy heart. King Saul vs. Jonathan

———

Is your heart healthy?

Hope and Faith

> "But I will hope continually, and will praise you yet more and more." (Psalm 71:14 NKJV)

———

> "Now may the God of hope fill you with all joy and peace in believing, that you may abound in hope by the power of the Holy Spirit." (Romans 15:13 NKJV)

———

> "For I know the thoughts that I think toward you, says the LORD, thoughts of peace and not of evil, to give you a future and a hope." (Jeremiah 29:11 NKJV)

Hope is our inheritance from God.

———

Guard your heart.

> "Above all else, guard your heart, for everything
> you do flows from it." (Proverbs 4:23)

Faith and Hope Under Fire

> "I have hidden your word in my heart that I might
> not sin against you." (Psalm 119:11)

DISCUSS

Take a few minutes with your group members to discuss what you just watched and explore these concepts together.

1. According to what you've heard today, how would you describe *faith*?

2. Reread 1 Samuel 14:1–14. Consider the stark contrast of faith between Jonathan and Saul. When have you been like King Saul, unwilling to get up and move forward, and when have you acted like Jonathan, boldly moving forward in faith?

3. How has your faith been *under fire*?

4. What gives you hope, even when your faith is being tested?

5. **Read James 1:1–5.** According to this passage, what else comes out of the testing of your faith?

6. How are you guarding your heart as you respond to the *three-mile walk*—God's call on your life?

RESPOND

Briefly review the outline for the video teaching and any notes you took. In the space below, write down the most significant point you took away from this session.

Is there a specific action step you can take this week to strengthen your faith, protect your heart, or move forward with hope as you respond to God's call?

PRAY

End the gathering by briefly sharing with your group one specific way they can pray for you this week. Pray that God would help you move forward with faith—individually and collectively—in the areas where he's calling you to take big leaps and small steps. Write down any specific requests in the space below so you can remember to continue praying throughout the week.

4

SESSION

—

Remember the story I shared during the video teaching about the house my wife and I bought recently? Thanks to a thorough home inspection, we discovered that half of our house was on a wooden foundation in desperate need of repair. For twenty-plus years, no one had bothered to check the foundation, which lacked ventilation and caused massive amounts of moisture to build up over time. Our home inspector discovered the wood was completely rotten and we had to replace all of it. This was our new home, and we had to replace the entire wooden section of the foundation (minus a portion of cement slab) to keep our home intact. I remind you of that story because I want you to do a little "home inspection" regarding the foundation of your faith over the next few days as you work through these daily exercises. And I want you to check the health of your heart as you thoughtfully consider your *Call to Faith.*

DAY 1: THE FOUR TRUTHS OF FAITH

Faith is the critical third mile on the journey of our *three-mile walk*. And here's what I know to be true about faith—based on my own life experience and my understanding of the way God talks about faith in the Scriptures:

1. We *all* have a measure of faith (Romans 12:3).
2. Our faith is powerful, no matter how small (Matthew 17:20).
3. Our faith grows as we use it (Ephesians 6:16).
4. God wants to help us with our faith, but we need to ask him (Mark 9:23–24).

These are what I consider the four truths of faith. And I believe these four truths are the good news of faith. Faith is a gift from God, and there is nothing we can do or *undo* about having faith. This is how incredible God is—He says, "You can't please me without faith, so I'm going to make sure you have faith." God gives us what we need to be successful as we follow his call. Not only does he give us faith, but God gives us faith powerful enough to move mountains. He says, "Whatever impossible situation you find yourself facing, you can move it with the faith you have—if you use it." Which is why our faith becomes active and grows the more we use it. Consider the shield, a tool or weapon that is only useful when you wield it. God says, "Whatever you use or steward or grow or develop in faith, that faith becomes strongly effective." But if we find ourselves in a place where our faith still seems small or weak or absent, then we can ask God for help. God is faithful to give us what we need on our own walk of faith. Consider your answers to the following questions regarding the way these truths show up in your life:

1. Read Romans 12:3–8. The first truth is that *we all have a measure of faith*. According to this passage, how did individual measures of faith contribute to the body of believers?

2. How has this been true for you—the idea that God has given you a measure of faith as you follow his call? Give an example.

3. Read Matthew 17:14–20. The second truth is that *our faith is powerful, no matter how small*. What is the significance of Jesus using the metaphor of a mustard seed as it relates to the size of faith?

4. How has this been true. for you—the idea that even a small amount of faith can move mountains and make the impossible possible? Give an example.

5. Read Ephesians 6:10–17. The third truth is that *our faith grows as we use it*. How is the shield different from the other pieces of armor? Why is action necessary to use a shield?

6. How has this been true for you—the idea that your faith grows the more you use it, the more you take action? Give an example.

7. **Read Mark 9:21–28.** The fourth truth is that *God wants to help us with our faith, but we need to ask him.* Why do you think God waits for us to ask for help?

8. How has this been true for you—the idea that God helps you when you ask him for help?

Read John 14:12–17a. This is what's possible with faith—*the impossible.* Jesus clearly tells his disciples that whomever believes in him will do even greater things. But it's not enough for them— or us—to know this; we have to have *faith* to believe this is true. Thank God for the promise of Jesus—that he will do whatever we ask in his name. And thank God for the gift of the Holy Spirit as your help and guide. Pray *in faith* for whatever it is you want God to do in your life right now, or for the courage and faith to step out into whomever God is asking you to be. Also pray not just for your own call to faith but also for the call to faith of those around you.

DAY 2: FAITH UNDER FIRE

Sincere faith isn't about being able to predict what God is going to do in our lives. It's about trusting God, knowing whatever he will do is what we want to do and where we want to be. But sometimes our faith goes *under fire*. Faith under fire is faith under pressure. It's those moments—in situations, circumstances, or relationships—when we're challenged at the very foundation of our faith. Pressure comes from different angles, both from others and from within ourselves. And when our faith is under fire, a few common questions start to flare:

- *Do I really believe God is who he says he is?*
- *Will God really do what he says he will do?*
- *Am I really who God says I am?*

What matters most in those moments is staying connected to God by reminding yourself of the four truths of faith, and by guarding your heart from the lies of the enemy. A healthy heart is what fuels your faith—*and* your courage as well as your pursuit of holiness. All three are necessary parts of the three-mile walk. And an unhealthy heart is what fuels evil and easily follows the lies of the enemy. May you take comfort in knowing you and I are not the only ones who have experienced faith under fire. Consider a few questions and passages of Scripture where faith was under fire for the prophets, disciples, and other followers of Jesus:

1. How has your faith been *under fire* lately?

2. **Read Daniel 3:17–18 and 26–27.** Daniel's faith was literally *under fire*. How did God respond to Daniel and his friends? How does this passage encourage your faith?

3. **Read Matthew 6:25–34.** Who were the people of "little faith" and how were they lacking faith? How does this passage encourage your faith?

4. **Read Matthew 8:23–27.** Why did the disciples have "little faith" in this situation? How does this passage encourage your faith?

5. **Read Matthew 16:5–12.** Why did the disciples have "little faith" in this situation? How does this passage encourage your faith?

6. How has God strengthened your faith from the fire or pressure you've experienced?

7. How have you seen someone else be strengthened by their own *faith under fire* experience?

8. If your faith were measured by what was coming out of your heart right now, would we see a healthy heart fueling faith or an unhealthy heart fueling lies and unbelief? Why?

Read Psalm 119:10–11. Time and time again, Scripture reminds us of the need to hide God's word in our hearts or guard our hearts by seeking after God, especially when we're under fire. Close today by asking God to give you a new perspective on what it means to guard your heart by seeking after him. Ask God to show you how to respond when your faith is under fire. Thank God for the promise of his presence at all times, and for the gift of faith that grows under fire.

DAY 3: SUPPLY LINE STRATEGY

Faith is our supply line, and in order for our faith to grow and be effective, we've got to maintain that supply line with strategy. I've mentioned the concept of a supply line strategy a few times now, especially if you're reading along in my book, *The Three-Mile Walk.* The supply line is extremely important for soldiers who are fighting behind a barricade or under siege because it is how soldiers get their food, medicine, and ammunition. If the supply line gets cut by the enemy—a common tactic of warfare—the situation becomes quite hopeless for the soldiers who are no longer receiving necessary aid. Perhaps this is how King Saul felt in 1 Samuel. King Saul was without a supply line of faith—operating from a place of fear and insecurity, and seemingly quite hopeless.

And yet Jonathan had a different response. I often wonder *what was it that led Jonathan to believe that he and one other guy had what it takes to go up against an army of thousands?* But I think Jonathan saw possibility when others saw impossibility because of his *faith.* Jonathan knew his faith in God was the supply line he needed to make the three-mile journey through the Valley of Mikmash (Michmash), and he did what he could to maintain and protect that supply line. While Jonathan most likely had physical supplies,

I believe maintaining a healthy heart of *hope* and *peace* were the supply line of his faith. This is what kept him and his armor-bearer operating from a place of security and peace, confident to move forward through the valley with God. And I believe hope and peace are the supply line to our faith too. We must build up, protect, and replenish the resources of hope and peace that fuel our faith. As you answer these questions, consider what it looks like for you to maintain a heart of hope and peace as your supply line strategy:

1. **Read Hebrews 1:11.** According to this verse, what is the definition of faith? How is hope vital to your faith?

2. Banning writes, "Hope is the pilot light in our hearts that ignites our faith" (page 144). If you want to continue growing in your faith, you must continue to hope. How do you stay hopeful?

3. **Read Romans 15:13.** How has God filled you with hope, joy, and peace in the past or present?

4. What effect did this have on your faith?

5. **Read Philippians 4:4–9.** What does this passage say about finding peace in God?

6. **Read John 16:33.** How does Jesus bring hope and peace to your life?

7. Where do you need more hope and peace in your life?

8. Maintaining a healthy heart is vital to every mile of the journey and is crucial to living with hope, peace, and faith. What is your strategy to maintaining a healthy heart so that you can move forward in faith?

Read Luke 6:43–49. Maintaining a supply line of faith, hope, and peace requires staying connected to God. This connection is what contributes to a healthy heart and a firm foundation. A healthy heart pours out good things—like hope and peace—and a healthy heart puts God's Word into practice. Faith is the fuel of a healthy heart, and the results of faith create a firm foundation. And yet, without a healthy heart, there is no faith and no firm foundation. Ask God to help you move forward in faith toward a healthy heart and by putting his words into practice. Thank God for the hope and peace that come from staying connected to his presence.

DAY 4: WAITING IN FAITH

One of the most important lessons in the *Call to Faith* is knowing that sometimes God asks us to wait *in faith*. This doesn't mean we sit down under a tree and wait passively like King Saul; or wait passively by scrolling on our phones like most of us do anytime we have a break in our schedule. Waiting in faith is very different than simply passing time. It's a posture of actively leaning forward in anticipation for something to come. It's the *qavah* kind of waiting from Hebrew, which means, "to wait, look for, hope, expect; to wait or look eagerly for, to lie in wait for, to wait, to linger for" (page 182 of *The Three-Mile Walk* book). It's the kind of waiting we do when we're expecting a special visitor to show up at our home and we frequently look out the window to see if they've arrived. It's the kind of waiting we did as a kid when we were told there would be a big surprise, so we kept eagerly searching and watching for that surprise. And this is what it looks like for us to wait in faith—to eagerly look for signs of God and what God has promised.

———

Read Hebrews 11. At the start of session four, we read the second half of "The Hall of Faith," but today I want you to read all of it from start to finish. As you meditate on this passage, use the space below to journal any thoughts, prayers, or ideas that come to mind. Make note of all the individuals who *waited in faith*. Which brief story most inspires you, and why?

FOR NEXT WEEK

Use the space below to write any key insights or questions from your personal study that you want to discuss at the next group meeting. In preparation for next week, review any highlights or notes you took in *The Three-Mile Walk*.

—

ENGAGING THE CALL

TAKE THE THREE-MILE

WALK WITH GOD—AND

DON'T MISS A MOMENT OF

BEING AND DOING WHAT

YOU WERE CREATED AND

CALLED TO BE AND DO.

Banning Liebscher

WELCOME

Children are the most persistent people on the planet. If you work with kids or live with kids, you know this well. You can tell them no, and five minutes later you're saying yes, simply because of their persistence. It's as if they are always on the lookout for opportunity, waiting in expectation for the next big moment or the next fun surprise. They're bold, they're confident, they're ready to take on the adventure of life, they have big goals, and they're not afraid to ask God for specific prayer requests while they dream big dreams. It's exhausting and inspiring all at the same time.

And before you know it, you're sitting in the passenger's seat teaching them to drive—the moment you wish their confidence was just a tad less bold behind the wheel. I remember sitting in the car with my oldest daughter, Elli, as she was working toward her driver's license. I was trying to teach her something, but she disagreed with me. "Elli, I've been driving for over twenty years, and you've been driving for three months," I said. She looked at me completely unimpressed and said, "Dad, I've been driving for *four* months." I didn't want to dim her confidence or make her scared of driving, but I did want her to understand the immense responsibility of driving a car. I wanted her to steward the power she possessed behind the wheel of a vehicle with responsibility and faithfulness. And that's how I feel about you too. I want you to understand the power you possess as you navigate your *three-mile walk* and as you engage God's call on your life.

I see so many adults today walking around unsatisfied, unfulfilled, looking for whatever it is they think they're missing. But what they're missing is life with God. They simply need to step out and engage the call of God in their lives. They need to be willing to risk it all, in order to find it all by following Jesus. Jesus gave his early disciples a call on their lives as "fishers of men," which was probably confusing and curious to a group of men who spent their lives catching fish. And yet, without knowing all the details, these men dropped their nets to follow Jesus. Jonathan, who was still young and inexperienced, risked his life alongside his friend, the armor-bearer, to hike three miles through a treacherous valley and go up against skilled soldiers because he knew God was with him.

So this is my heart for you as we close out this study—that you would be aware of God's presence at all times, that you would be willing to drop it all, and that you would live a life fully alive in your relationship with Jesus by *engaging your call*. This is *the three-mile walk*.

SHARE

Begin your group time by inviting anyone to share their insights from last week's personal study. Next, to kick things off, discuss one of the following questions:

- When you hear the word *responsibility*, what comes to mind?
  — *or* —
- If you could unload a few of your responsibilities or pass them off to someone else, which would be your top two to unload, and why?

READ

Invite someone to read aloud the following passage. Listen for fresh insight and to share any new thoughts with the group through the questions that follow.

The First Disciples

When Jesus heard that John had been put in prison, he withdrew to Galilee. Leaving Nazareth, he went and lived in Capernaum, which was by the lake in the area of Zebulun and Naphtali—to fulfill what was said through the prophet Isaiah:

"Land of Zebulun and land of Naphtali,
   the Way of the Sea, beyond the Jordan,
   Galilee of the Gentiles—
the people living in darkness
   have seen a great light;
on those living in the land of the shadow
      of death
   a light has dawned."

From that time on Jesus began to preach, "Repent, for the kingdom of heaven has come near." As Jesus was walking beside the Sea of Galilee, he saw two brothers, Simon called Peter and his brother Andrew. They were casting a net into the lake, for they were fishermen. "Come, follow me," Jesus said, "and I will send you out to fish for people." At once they left their nets and followed him. Going on from there, he saw two other brothers, James son of Zebedee and his brother John. They were in a boat with their father Zebedee, preparing their nets. Jesus called them, and immediately they left the boat and their father and followed him. (Matthew 4:12-22).

What is one key insight that stands out to you from this passage?

Why do you think the disciples were willing to *immediately* follow Jesus? How do you think this disrupted their lives?

WATCH

Play the video for session five. As you and your group watch, use the following outline to record any thoughts or key points that stand out to you.

Notes

Engaging the Call of God Is Born from a Place of Responsibility

Jonathan's sense of responsibility.

Living with a sense of responsibility means being willing to sacrifice.

The responsibility of followers of Jesus:

- take care of the poor
- share your faith
- be generous
- pray
- take care of orphans and widows

The journey begins with a sense of responsibility and the journey is sustained with a sense of responsibility.

Following God Is Your Responsibility

We will experience fulfilment and satisfaction when we understand our responsibilities.

You were created to follow Jesus.

Jesus doesn't call us with details, he calls us with a promise.

"Follow me, and I will make you fishers of men." (Matthew 4:19 NKJV)

The promise of Jesus.

Victory for Jonathan and the Israelites.

DISCUSS

Take a few minutes with your group members to discuss what you just watched and explore these concepts together.

1. What stands out to you in today's teaching? How can you relate to Banning's message?

2. **Read Matthew 27:11–26.** How is the response of Pilate similar to King Saul's as it relates to their responsibilities?

3. Is there any area in your life where you sense you need to reclaim responsibility?

4. Reread 1 Samuel 14:11–23. How did Jonathan's sense of responsibility influence the responsibility of the rest of the Israelite army, including King Saul?

5. What sense of responsibility are you leaning into today as you engage the call of God in your life? And what steps will you take or changes will you make to lean into those responsibilities?

6. Where do you need encouragement as you engage the call of God in your life? And what will you do to encourage someone else on their journey, too?

RESPOND

Briefly review the outline for the video teaching and any notes you took. In the space below, write down the most significant point you took away from this session.

Take inventory of your responsibilities. Are you carrying a few extra responsibilities that are not yours to carry? If so, how will you let go of those responsibilities?

PRAY

End the gathering by praying for one another. Pray especially that God would help each one of you live boldly and dream big as you engage God's call in your life. Pray for holiness, courage, and faith to live the life God has for you, as individuals and as a community. Write down any specific requests in the space below so you can remember to continue praying throughout the week.

FINAL
PERSONAL STUDY

5

SESSION

If you've ever run a long-distance race, you know the most important skill to have near the end of the race isn't speed; it's stamina. I'm sure Jonathan could tell us a lot about stamina on this last leg of the three-mile walk if he were here with us today. And stamina is what you will also need in this moment. We're finished with our group discussions for this study, and yet the remaining work on the following pages is *just* as important as the work you've done until now. Engaging in God's call isn't just *one* three-mile walk—it's a lifetime of three-mile walks adding up to a lifetime of long-distance journeys. If your stamina is low, lean into the stamina of God. And let this be our prayer together,

"I thank my God every time I remember you. In all my prayers for all of you, I always pray with joy because of your partnership in the gospel from the first day until now, being confident of this, that he who began a good work in you will carry it on to completion until the day of Christ Jesus." (Philippians 1:3–6).

God continues to do a good work in you, so keep up your pace and stay with me as we look at what it means for you to continue engaging his call in your life. Here we go!

DAY 1: NOW IS YOUR MOMENT

I know you may be sitting here thinking, *This is great stuff, Banning! I just need a little bit more time to figure out my call or plan out how I will respond to the dreams and desires God has given me.* And my answer to you is *get moving.* Now is your moment. Not later, not tomorrow, not next year. *Now.* Consider Jonathan at the moment we find him in 1 Samuel 14. Jonathan, his father, and their terrified army of six hundred men are huddled in their camp waiting for the arrival of "thirty thousand chariots and six thousand horsemen, and people as the sand [is] on the seashore" (1 Samuel 13:5). Talk about a *moment.*

This was Jonathan's moment of opportunity for faith. And my guess is that you've had plenty of those moments of opportunities of faith too. Moments when you have had a split second to decide if you're going to respond in anger or love, entitlement or gratitude, ignorance or honesty, power or influence, harshness or gentleness, fear or faith. Often, in those moments, we decide how to respond based on repetition. Repeated experience tells our brains to pay attention and keep that information in a retrievable place, because we will probably need it again. This means repetition can be naturally built into our experiences over time and it can also be created by our choices. This *also* means we have a degree of control over how we react or respond to moments of crisis and the everyday moments of our lives. We can choose to respond *with* God or *without* God. Consider how God's presence and promises influence the way you *live in the moment* as you engage God's call in your life.

1. Have you ever been faced with a big moment or split-second decision like the one Jonathan must have been experiencing?

2. How do you stay present in the moment? (*I recognize this is a discipline for those of us who prefer replaying past moments or anticipating future moments.*)

3. What practices or repetitions have been helpful for you in *responding*, rather than *reacting*, during moments of crisis?

4. **Read Luke 9:57–62.** Why do you think Jesus requires an immediate response of the disciples, whom he asked to follow him?

5. **Read Matthew 8:13; Matthew 9:22; Matthew 15:28; and Matthew 17:18 in the NIV translation.** What is the common phrase at the end of each verse? Why do you think Jesus allows people to be healed quickly versus healing people over time?

6. Read Philippians 4:19 in the NKJV translation. How does this promise help us live in the moment?

7. Is there anything holding you back from responding to God's call on your life in this moment? (*We can be held back by feeling like we're not ready, by our feelings of responsibility for someone else's "moment," by relationships, fears, past failures, insecurity, by the grief of letting go of our own dreams or desires when they are different from what God has for us, and so on.*)

8. How will you decide to live in the moment—God's moment for you—today?

Read Galatians 2:19–20. If it is Christ who lives in us, then we can stand confident and secure as we live and respond in the moment. And we can trust God to give us grace when we miss a moment or mess up. Ask God to help you remember to rely on him in every moment. Thank God for his presence with you as you engage his call in your life.

DAY 2: PRACTICING THE DISCIPLINES

One of the things rock climbers use to be successful and safe in their climbs are anchors to secure themselves to a rock face. Professional climbers are trained to look for natural anchors in the rock, as well as use their own artificial anchors. Once tested and secure, these anchors allow the climbers to move up the surface of a rock with confidence, knowing that if they slip and fall, the anchor will hold them.

This is how I view the spiritual disciplines—as anchors for our journey with God. Unfortunately, many Christians today perceive spiritual disciplines as religious rituals and either don't engage them or just go through the motions because they know these practices are the "right" things to do. So, we pray, read our Bibles, attend church and sing worship songs out of duty and expectation. But if we want to live an awakened life and engage God's call in our lives, then we need the spiritual disciplines as anchors.

We need to be feeding ourselves a steady diet of truth by reading, studying, meditating on, praying and declaring the Word of God. We can do this in many forms and venues—privately with our own Bibles and study tools, in small groups, at church, on our smartphones, or in a more formal setting like Bible or ministry school. I believe the spiritual disciplines, when used properly, are part of our supply line strategy to stay connected to the heart of God—they anchor our hearts with hope and peace, which fuels our faith on the journey. Practicing the disciplines is one of the most important ways we engage God's call and grow our faith on the *three-mile walk.* Consider what spiritual disciplines look like in your own life as you answer these questions:

1. Have you ever tried rock-climbing? If so, what was that experience like for you?

2. **Read Hebrews 10:24–25.** How do you think the first Christians practiced spiritual disciplines? Why were the disciplines important to them?

3. Do you remember your earliest experience learning about or actually practicing the spiritual disciplines? If so, what was that experience like for you?

4. How are spiritual disciplines encouraged and practiced in your faith community today?

5. Which disciplines are most meaningful to you right now on your *three-mile walk?* Why?

6. What other "anchors" do you turn to if you're not practicing spiritual disciplines? Are these anchors helpful? Why or why not?

7. **Read 2 Timothy 1:6–14 in the NIV translation.** According to this passage, what does the Spirit of God give us (see verse 7)? And how do the disciplines help us "guard the good deposit" that was entrusted to us (see verse 14)?

8. What noticeable difference does it make to practice the spiritual disciplines on your *three-mile walk* as you engage the call of God in your life?

9. Read the passages where various spiritual disciplines are referenced. Then pick one of these disciplines and put it into practice today. Ask God for help if you're struggling to be consistent or having a hard time finding space to practice.

- Prayer–1 Thessalonians 5:17
- Bible Reading–Psalm 119:11
- Sabbath–Exodus 16:23
- Community–Hebrews 10:25
- Celebration–Acts 4:21
- Worship–Matthew 26:30
- Silence–1 Samuel 3:9
- Solitude—Mark 1:35
- Service—John 13:12–14

For a comprehensive list of spiritual disciplines, check out *Spiritual Disciplines Handbook: Practices That Transform Us* by Adele Ahlberg Calhoun (Downers Grove, IL: InterVarsity Press, 2015, revised and expanded in 2015).

DAY 3: FINDING JOY IN THE MIDDLE SEAT

Some of you may have noticed how I left *Thanksgiving* out of the spiritual disciplines list on Day Two. It's because we're going to camp out on this very important practice today. But first, a brief story. A few years ago, I found myself on a last-minute cross-country flight, crammed into the middle seat of the last row with limited leg room and no ability to recline. This was definitely not an ideal scenario for a tall guy on a five-hour flight. Needless to say, I was irritated and annoyed. I threw a pity party for myself, lost perspective, became ungrateful, and felt entitled about something as trivial as a seat on an airplane. And then I realized how ridiculous I was being. I thought about the people I know serving around the world in less-than-ideal circumstances, risking their lives to bring the good news of the gospel in challenging places and spaces. And here I was, stewing over a small inconvenience.

This experience shaped me in significant ways that influence the way I lead and live today. The lesson I learned was about "finding joy in the middle seat," and what I mean by this is keeping a perspective of gratitude in every situation in which we find ourselves. Giving thanks is an essential spiritual practice on the *three-mile walk*. It's another supply line strategy for infusing hope, peace, and joy in order to fuel our faith for the long haul of our journey with God. Continually giving thanks helps us see God's bigger purpose in times of trial, and it helps us act with faith in every circumstance. Finding joy in the middle seat allows us to recognize that problems are opportunities for God to show up, so that we face them with a heart of thanksgiving. Consider what this looks like for you by answering these questions:

1. Do you have a recent story similar to Banning's, where you were irritated and annoyed by a small inconvenience?

2. How do you maintain an attitude of thanksgiving amidst frustrating circumstances—like the middle seat of an airplane?

3. **Read 1 Thessalonians 5:18.** Is there someone in your life who gives thanks in all circumstances? What is it like to be around that person?

4. What are a few practical ways you express gratitude toward God on a regular basis?

5. **Read Psalm 100.** How does King David express thanksgiving to God? How do *you* participate in this expression?

6. Is there a particular area of your life where you're struggling, irritated, or annoyed right now? How does giving thanks in that area shift your perspective from negative to positive?

7. Read 1 Corinthians 1:4–9. According to this passage, why is Paul grateful? How does Paul's gratitude point to what God is doing?

8. How do you express your gratitude to others? How can you take a cue from Paul and specifically point someone to God with a few words of thanksgiving today?

Read 2 Thessalonians 1. This letter is an expression of gratitude to the Thessalonians because of their perseverance of faith. Imagine being one of the Thessalonians and hearing this letter after enduring a really hard season of life. How encouraged they must have felt, knowing their circumstances were not in vain—knowing their situation resulted in noticeable growth and increased love toward one another. Consider how Paul's words in this passage encourage your heart too. Thank God for the gift of your circumstances because of the gifts of growth, love, and perseverance you've received. Ask God to show you the joy of giving thanks in all circumstances. And thank God for his presence and grace even when you forget to give thanks.

DAY 4: LIVING A BOLD LIFE

If you look at all the great heroes of faith in the Bible, they all had moments where they spoke up and declared God's word over a situation. Their boldness to speak up ushered in the awareness of God's plans and literally changed history. And by boldness, I mean "freedom in speaking, free and fearless confidence, cheerful courage, confidence" (page 181 of the *Three-Mile Walk* book).

When we speak bold words of faith and choose to live a bold life today, we too partner with the plans and purposes of God. There is a great boldness that comes when we say what God has said and done—or what he is doing and saying—in our lives, because it shows we are confident that God will back up his Word. When we declare the promises and testimonies of God in faith over a situation, we release power for God to come and do it again, and again. This is the boldness of faith.

The book of Acts tells us of the boldness of Peter and John in front of the rulers, elders, and scribes of their day. "Now when they saw the boldness of Peter and John, and perceived they were uneducated and untrained men, they marveled. And they realized that they had been with Jesus" (Acts 4:13). This is the benefit of living a BOLD life—that people look at our boldness and know we follow Jesus. And this is how we live a bold life—*by awakening our hearts to the call of God in our lives, and by engaging that call.*

Read Luke 8:35–43. This is the story of a blind man named Bartimaeus whose place in time and history relegated him to the life of a beggar. Without any means to contribute to society, he provided for himself and his family by sitting and begging for alms on the outskirts of the city. That is, until he met Jesus. As you meditate on this passage, use the space below to journal any thoughts, prayers, or ideas that come to mind. Make note of how Bartimaeus waited and responded to Jesus in bold faith. How does this story inspire you?

FINISH STRONG

Use the space below to write any key insights or questions from your personal study that you want to discuss if your group decides to continue meeting. Otherwise, visit JesusCulture.com for additional resources from Banning Liebscher.

Epilogue

Some of the best advice I've been given in living out God's call in my life is to be specific with my prayers. I truly believe bold faith is *specific*. However, most of us are afraid to be specific because we're afraid of failure or we're trying to avoid disappointment in our lives or the lives of others. When we live our lives avoiding failure, we stay general. We stay general in our dreams, in our goals, and in our prayer requests that way we can avoid the possibility of God not responding to our specific desires. But without specific prayers of faith, we never get to see specific answers that grow our faith.

Getting specific shows God that we are willing to risk certain things to see him show up on our behalf. We need to be specific if we're going to live with bold faith. And we need to be specific if we're going to engage God's call in our lives in a way that aligns our dreams and desires with God's dreams and desires for us. So, here is my specific promise to you: I will consistently pray for each one of you as you work through this material.

> I will pray that your heart will be awakened to God's call in your life.
> I will pray for specific dreams and desires for you.
> I will pray that the purpose of your three-mile walk will be clear to you.

I will pray that you have the desire, the courage, and the faith to keep moving forward.

I will pray for moments of bold faith.

I will pray for peace and clarity as you practice the spiritual disciplines.

I will pray that you cling to God's promises for you.

I will pray for a heart of gratitude for you.

This will be my prayer as God reminds me of all of you. May you be awakened, challenged, changed, and transformed by God's promises and God's presence on your *three-mile walk* with him.

Grace and peace,
—*Banning*

Leader's Guide

Thank you for your willingness to lead your group through this study! What you have chosen to do is valuable and will make a great difference in the lives of others. The rewards of being a leader are different from those of participating, and we hope that as you lead you will find your own walk with Jesus deepened by this experience.

The Three-Mile Walk is a five-session study built around video content and small-group interaction. As the group leader, just think of yourself as the host of a dinner party. Your job is to take care of your guests by managing all the behind-the-scenes details, so that when everyone arrives, they can just enjoy time together.

As the group leader, your role is not to answer all the questions or reteach the content—the video, book, and study guide will do most of that work. Your job is to guide the experience and cultivate your small group into a kind of teaching community. This will make it a place for members to process, question, and reflect—not receive more instruction.

Before your first meeting, make sure everyone in the group gets a copy of the study guide. This will keep everyone on the same page and help the process run more smoothly. If some group members are unable to purchase the guide, arrange it so that people can share the resource with other group members. Giving everyone access to all the material will position this study to be as rewarding an experience as possible. Everyone should feel free to write in his or her study guide and bring it to group every week.

SETTING UP THE GROUP

You will need to determine with your group how long you want to meet each week so you can plan your time accordingly. Generally, most groups like to meet for either ninety minutes or two hours, so you could use one of the following schedules:

SECTION	90 MINUTES	120 MINUTES
Welcome (members arrive and get settled)	10 minutes	15 minutes
Share (discuss one or more of the opening questions for the session)	10 minutes	15 minutes
Read (discuss the questions based on the Scripture reading for the week)	10 minutes	15 minutes
Watch (watch the teaching material together and take notes)	20 minutes	20 minutes
Discuss (discuss the Bible study questions you selected ahead of time)	30 minutes	40 minutes
Respond / Pray (pray together as a group and dismiss)	10 minutes	15 minutes

As the group leader, you'll want to create an environment that encourages sharing and learning. A church sanctuary or formal classroom may not be as ideal as a living room, because those locations can feel formal and less intimate. No matter what setting you choose, provide enough comfortable seating for everyone, and, if possible, arrange the seats in a semicircle so everyone can see the video easily. This will make transition between the video and group conversation more efficient and natural.

Also, try to get to the meeting site early so you can greet participants as they arrive. Simple refreshments create a welcoming atmosphere and can be a wonderful addition to a group study evening. Try to take food and pet allergies into account to make your guests as comfortable as possible. You may also want to consider offering childcare to couples with children who want to attend. Finally, be sure your media technology is working properly. Managing these details up front will make the rest of your group experience flow smoothly and provide a welcoming space in which to engage the content of *The Three-Mile Walk*.

STARTING THE GROUP TIME

Once everyone has arrived, it's time to begin the group. Here are some simple tips to make your group time healthy, enjoyable, and effective.

First, begin the meeting with a short prayer and remind the group members to put their phones on silent. This is a way to make sure you can all be present with one another and with God. Next, give each person a few minutes to respond to the questions in the "Share" and "Read" sections. This won't require as much time in session one, but beginning in session two, people will need more time to share their insights from their personal studies. Usually, you won't answer the discussion questions yourself, but you should go first with the "Share" and "Read" questions, answering briefly and with a reasonable amount of transparency.

At the end of session one, invite the group members to complete the between-sessions personal studies for that week. Explain that you will be providing some time before the video teaching next week for anyone to share insights. Let them know sharing is optional, and it's no problem if they can't get to some of the between-sessions activities some weeks. It will still be beneficial for them to hear from the other participants and learn about what they discovered.

LEADING THE DISCUSSION TIME

Now that the group is engaged, it's time to watch the video and respond with some directed small-group discussion. Encourage all the group members to participate in the discussion, but make sure they know they don't have to do so. As the discussion progresses, you may want to follow up with comments such as, "Tell me more about that," or, "Why did you answer that way?" This will allow the group participants to deepen their reflections and invite meaningful sharing in a nonthreatening way.

Note that you have been given multiple questions to use in each session, and you do not have to use them all or even follow them in order. Feel free to pick and choose questions based on either the needs of your group or how the conversation is flowing. Also, don't be afraid of silence. Offering a question and allowing up to thirty seconds of silence is okay. It allows people space to think about how they want to respond and also gives them time to do so.

As group leader, you are the boundary keeper for your group. Do not let anyone (yourself included) dominate the group time.

Keep an eye out for group members who might be tempted to "attack" folks they disagree with or try to "fix" those having struggles. These kinds of behaviors can derail a group's momentum, so they need to be steered in a different direction. Model active listening and encourage everyone in your group to do the same. This will make your group time a safe space and create a positive community.

The group discussion leads to a closing time of individual reflection and prayer. Encourage the participants to take a few moments to review what they've learned during the session and write down their thoughts to the "Respond" section. This will help them cement the big ideas in their minds as you close the session. Conclude by having the participants break into smaller groups of two to three people to pray for one another.

Thank you again for taking the time to lead your group. You are making a difference in the lives of others and having an impact on the kingdom of God!

The Three-Mile Walk

The Courage You Need to Live the Life God Wants for You

Banning Liebscher

We are all called to be change-makers in the world, and yet many of us don't know how to answer the call. Jesus Culture founder and pastor Banning Liebscher reveals the three key moves that will awaken your heart and propel you into a life of divine purpose.

You were made for more than a life of holy discontent—more than the frustrating sense of sitting on the sidelines of your own life's purpose. From the beginning, Jesus has beckoned us out of passivity and into a high-stakes adventure with hearts fully alive, lives fully engaged, and the courage needed for both.

With a heart-stirring message and compelling stories, Liebscher will equip you with practical guidance to be and do all that God has called you to. *The Three-Mile Walk* draws from the biblical story of Jonathan, who, after a treacherous three-mile hike, boldly stepped into battle and watched God work a stunning victory in the midst of impossible odds. Likewise, Liebscher presents the three key attributes you need to fully engage your mission—courage, holiness, and faith. In his power-packed, memorable style, Liebscher offers fresh insight and instruction for answering your calling with a courageous "yes," and setting out on the journey of a lifetime.

You are meant to change the world. It's going to be tough, surprising, and more fulfilling than you can imagine. You just need the courage to rise up and walk it out.

Available in stores and online!

ZONDERVAN®
.com